UNFORGETTABLE
NEWS REPORTS

TIME
For Kids

Tamara Leigh Hollingsworth

Consultants

Timothy Rasinski, Ph.D.
Kent State University

Lori Oczkus
Literacy Consultant

Based on writing from
TIME For Kids. TIME For Kids and the *TIME
For Kids* logo are registered trademarks of
TIME Inc. Used under license.

Publishing Credits

Dona Herweck Rice, *Editor-in-Chief*
Lee Aucoin, *Creative Director*
Jamey Acosta, *Senior Editor*
Heidi Fiedler, *Editor*
Lexa Hoang, *Designer*
Stephanie Reid, *Photo Editor*
Rachelle Cracchiolo, *M.S.Ed., Publisher*

Image Credits: Cover, p.1 Getty Images;
pp.44–45 Jeff Widener/Associated Press;
p.13 Public Domain; pp.4–5, 7, 32–33 (top),
34–35, 38–39, 42 (left), 44–45 (top), 48–49,
49 (top), 50, 50–51, 53 (third from top), 54,
55 (right) Getty Images; pp.9 (bottom), 10,
16, 17 (middle), 20, 28 (top), 30, 33 (bottom)
The Granger Collection; pp.11, 12, 17 (top,
bottom), 18–19, 23–24, 26, 28 (bottom),
31–33 (middle), 41 (top), 51 (bottom), 53
(top, bottom) The Library of Congress;
p.8 Massachusetts Historical Society;
p.53 (second from top) Picture History/
Newscom; pp.29 (left), 42 (right), 42–43, 43
NASA; pp.3–4 NOAA; pp.14–15 (illustrations)
John Scahill & Timothy J. Bradley; All other
images from Shutterstock.

Teacher Created Materials

5301 Oceanus Drive
Huntington Beach, CA 92649-1030
http://www.tcmpub.com
ISBN 978-1-4333-4945-4

TABLE OF CONTENTS

THAT'S NEWS TO ME!

There are all kinds of news. There's family news, school news, **local** news, and world news. Some news makes us happy. Other news makes us sad or worried. News happens everywhere, every day. Today, people learn about news almost as soon as it happens. It's easy to stay well informed.

THINK LINK

> What are some of history's most unforgettable news stories?

> How does the way we learn about news change how we understand events?

> In what ways might we get news in the future?

online

News

technolo...

travel

For thousands of years, the only news people heard was local news. But over time, new ways of spreading news were developed. The world's greatest events have been reported in many ways. But our desire to know what is happening has never changed. From local feuds to the birth of a new king, it has always been important to follow the news. And whenever or wherever it happens, the most powerful news is unforgettable.

OLD NEWS

The first newspapers appeared as early as the Roman Empire. Julius Caesar, the Roman Emperor, ordered that the events of the empire be announced along with information about births, marriages, and deaths.

Chiusa la
regolare,

Up in Smoke

Some ancient civilizations used drumbeats or smoke signals to communicate across great distances. But this wasn't always the best method. Weather could interfere with these messages. And if there weren't clear lines of sight between the two sides, some information would be lost.

THE POWER OF THE PRESS

The game Telephone is played with a group of friends. One person whispers a piece of news to the next person. The last person in the circle says the news aloud. The fun comes at the end of the game when everyone hears how crazy the message has become.

During the 1700s, news traveled in the same way. Reports came **orally**, or by word of mouth. But oral news isn't always reliable. Mistakes can happen if someone hears the message incorrectly. Details can be forgotten. In the 1700s, many people didn't know how to read. Printing presses existed, but they were hard to use. There were few daily papers. Oral news wasn't perfect, but it was the most common way to learn about the latest events.

EXTRA! EXTRA!

The *New England Courant* was one of the first newspapers printed in the United States. It was founded and published by Benjamin Franklin's brother James. It was modeled after a newspaper in England called *The Spectator*. It contained articles, **editorials**, and humorous writings.

START THE PRESSES!

Before the year 1440, most books were handwritten. In 1440, Johannes Gutenburg made a machine with moveable type that pressed ink down on a page like a stamp. Before the printing press, most people couldn't read. But when books became easier to make, **literacy** rates rose across Europe.

Printers review work done on an early printing press.

Revolutionary Lights

During the Revolutionary War, colonists passed news orally. The British were planning a surprise attack. They would be coming from Boston. A man watched for signs of the troops. He would shine one lantern if the troops were marching across the land. If they rowed across the river, he would shine two lanterns. It took less than a minute to identify the signal. Several messengers set out to warn that the British army was on its way. The most famous of these was Paul Revere.

FACT VS. FICTION

Revere is popularly imagined yelling his warning, "The British are coming!" In truth, he went knocking door to door. Since people were asleep, they may not have heard him if he quickly rode by their house. And he didn't want to be caught or captured by British patrols, so he avoided drawing attention to himself with loud shouts.

SOUND THE ALARM

The saying "one if by land, two if by sea" is a line from a famous poem. *Paul Revere's Ride* is a poem by Henry Wadsworth Longfellow. The saying comes from the section of the poem reprinted below.

PAUL REVERE'S RIDE.

LISTEN, my children, and you shall hear
Of the midnight ride of Paul Revere,
On the eighteenth of April, in Seventy-five;
Hardly a man is now alive
Who remembers that famous day and year.

He said to his friend, "If the British march
By land or sea from the town to-night,
Hang a lantern aloft in the belfry-arch
Of the North Church tower as a signal light,—
One, if by land, and two, if by sea;
And I on the opposite shore will be,
Ready to ride and spread the alarm

Wise Words

It took more than word of mouth for the Revolutionary War to get started. In 1776, Thomas Paine published a small 50-page booklet. The **pamphlet**, *Common Sense*, explained Paine's ideas. He wanted the British to let the colonists rule themselves. It was dangerous to print these ideas. So Paine published the pamphlet without his name on it. The pamphlet quickly sold over 500,000 copies. It helped people understand the ideas behind the revolution.

COMMON SENSE;

ADDRESSED TO THE

INHABITANTS

OF

AMERICA,

On the following interesting

SU

MDCCLXXVI.

SPREADING THE WORD

Paine's words helped many people realize the importance of their independence and persuaded Americans to fight for their freedom. Later, his writings helped persuade the people of France to do the same.

seamstress and patriot Betsy Ross, believed by many to have sewn the first American flag

American CRISIS.

NUMBER II.

BY THE AUTHOR OF

COMMON SENSE.

PHIL A

Printed and Sold

Second-ftreet,

[Price *Four-pence* fingle

Where alfo may be had

IN CRISIS

Thomas Paine also wrote *The American Crisis*. This collection of essays impacted many people. As in *Common Sense*, Paine used words that were easy to understand. The essays were meant to inspire men to fight in the war.

THE PRINTING PRESS

Today, you can press a few keys and words pop up on a computer screen. Click *send* and your words can be sent instantly to anyone, anywhere in the world. Press *print* and your words can be seen on a sheet of paper. Amazing! Hundreds of years ago, people thought a printing press was amazing. And it was, compared to writing out each copy by hand. But it wasn't nearly as easy as a computer.

1

Each press required hundreds of metal letters, numbers, and punctuation marks. Each symbol was raised on a small piece of metal. Flat pieces were used for the spaces between the words.

2

Letters were arranged in a row in a narrow tray. Each line of text was placed into a frame for printing. Black ink was spread on the raised areas of each metal piece. Once the letters and ink were prepared, they were rolled into the press.

The average printing press was nearly as large as a twin bed.

3 A heavy block was rotated down onto the paper. It pressed the metal letters into the paper to transfer the ink. Multiple copies could be made. When a section was completed, each letter was cleaned and used again to form new lines of type.

FIGHTING WORDS

By the mid 1800s, many things had changed about the way people got information. Word of mouth was no longer the standard. Print had become the best way to share news. It was easy and cheap. Newspapers could be printed daily. But reporters still had trouble traveling. In most cases, papers only covered local events. During the Civil War, people sought the news to help them understand events across the nation. Letters and books helped people form their beliefs about the war.

sheet music from the Civil War

NORTH OR SOUTH

During the war, the southern states formed the **Confederacy**. Those states wanted to break away from the country. The northern states were called the Union because they wanted the country to remain unified.

DIXIE DOODLE,

A SONG

Written, Composed and Dedicated

"Our dear Soldiers on the

BY

Mrs. Margaret

NEW ORLEANS
PUBLISHED BY P. P. WERLEIN

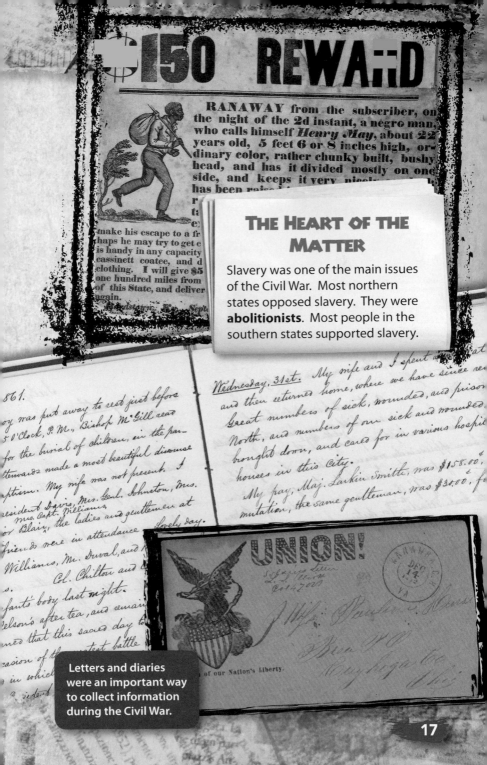

$150 REWARD

RANAWAY from the subscriber, on the night of the 2d instant, a negro man, who calls himself *Henry May*, about 22 years old, 5 feet 6 or 8 inches high, ordinary color, rather chunky built, bushy head, and has it divided mostly on one side, and keeps it very nicely

make his escape to a fr...
...haps he may try to get e...
is handy in any capacity...
cassinett coatee, and d...
clothing. I will give $5...
one hundred miles from...
of this State, and deliver...
again.

THE HEART OF THE MATTER

Slavery was one of the main issues of the Civil War. Most northern states opposed slavery. They were **abolitionists**. Most people in the southern states supported slavery.

Letters and diaries were an important way to collect information during the Civil War.

A Powerful Story

In 1852, *Uncle Tom's Cabin* was published. Harriet Beecher Stowe, the author, wanted to end slavery. She wrote the book to help spread her ideas. The novel was about the life of a slave named Uncle Tom. The book helped people understand the difficult lives of slaves. Much like the pamphlet *Common Sense*, the printing of *Uncle Tom's Cabin* helped change the world. Abraham Lincoln said it was the novel that "started the Great War."

Harriet Beecher Stowe

UNCLE TOM'S CABIN

"There have been great societies that did not use the wheel, but there have been no societies that did not tell stories."

—Ursula K. LeGuin, writer

IN HIS OWN WORDS

The *Narrative of the Life of Frederick Douglass* was written by Frederick Douglass, a man who escaped from slavery. He wrote about his life so others would see what it was like to be a slave.

President Abraham Lincoln listening to Frederick Douglass

Writing Home

Before there were TVs or radios, letters were a popular way to share news. The stories they told were personal. During the Civil War, people counted on letters to get news of the war. But paper was expensive. And during the war, there was little extra money to go around. So letters were few and far between. Family members waited anxiously for mail. They hoped to hear news of their loved ones in battle. Some letters were filled with words of passion and hope. Others were **pessimistic** and sad.

Today, the National Postal Museum in Washington, DC displays some Civil-War-era letters that give a glimpse into the lives and feelings of Americans during this difficult time.

LOVE LETTERS

Mail service during this time wasn't as **consistent** as it is today. People often waited weeks to get news from loved ones.

Remember to Write that Letter Home!

Staying in touch with home seems even more important during times of war as shown by these soldiers during World War I.

FLAG OF TRUCE

During the worst days of the war, mail delivery was officially stopped in the southern states. But people set up the flag of **truce** system. The flag was a sign that letter carriers were not involved in the fighting. In this way, people could still write and communicate with each other.

TRAVELERS' TALES

Farmers who owned huge pieces of land lived far away from towns. They still depended on oral news. When traveling preachers or salesmen visited, the farmers heard news from all the places the men had been.

CIVIL WAR LETTERS

We know about the battles, the deaths, and the weapons of the Civil War. But through letters, we also know how it felt to live through the war. Each letter tells a different tale of what life was like during the war. The letters are now **artifacts**, safely stored in museums around the country. But the beauty of the written word is that it can be re-created for others to read.

A LETTER FROM POET WALT WHITMAN TO MR. AND MRS. S. B. HASKELL

Washington August 10 1863

Mr and Mrs Haskell,

Dear friends, I thought it would be soothing to you to have a few lines about the last days of your son Erastus Haskell of Company K, 141st New York Volunteers. I write in haste, & nothing of importance—only I thought any thing about Erastus would be welcome. From the time he came to Armory Square Hospital till he died, there was hardly a day but I was with him a portion of the time—if not during the day, then at night. I had no opportunity to do much, or any thing for him, as nothing was needed, only to wait the progress of his malady. I am only a friend, visiting the wounded & sick soldiers, (not connected with any society—or State.) From the first I felt that Erastus was in danger, or at least was much worse than they in the hospital supposed. As he made no complaint, they perhaps [thought him] not very bad—I told the [doctor of the ward] to look him over again—he was a much [sicker boy?] than he supposed, but he took it lightly...

STOP! THINK...

- What is Whitman writing about?

- How do you think Erastus's family felt when they received the letter?

- Have you ever received important news in a letter?

Mr & Mrs _____

Dear friends, I thought it would be soothing to you to have a few lines about the last days of your son Erastus Haskell of Company K 141st New York Volunteers. I write in haste, & nothing of importance — only I thought any thing about Erastus would be welcome. From the time he came to Armory Square Hospital till he died, there was hardly a day but I was with him a portion of the time — if not during the day, then at night. I had no opportunity to do much, or any thing for him, as was needed, only to wait the progress of his malady. I am a friend visiting the wounded & sick soldiers (not connected with any society—or State.) From the first I felt that he was in danger, or at least was much worse than the hospital supposed. As he made no complaint, they perhaps ...him nothing but bad. I told the the ward over ...them, he was a much sicker he supposed, but he took it lightly, said, I K about these fever cases them you do — the you ...sick, but I shall certainly bring him out of I have no doubt the doctor meant well & did any rate, about a week or so before Erastus really alarmed & after that he & all the do help him, but without avail — May be ...have made any difference any how — I th ...was broken down, poor boy, before he came to here — I believe he came here about July 11th I took to him, he was a quiet young man, correct & decent said little — I used to sit his bed — I said once, You don't talk ...leave me to do all the talking — he on I was never much of a talker. The do ...one to cheer him up very lively — I was a ...cheerful with him, but did not feel to be ...I tried to tell him some amusing narrat ...minutes I stopt, I saw that the effect

HELLO, WORLD

With the invention of the telegraph and telephone, people no longer had to wait for the news. They could learn the latest events in minutes, sometimes seconds. These new ways of spreading information were **vital** during World War I. Important events were reported to newspapers in telegrams. People were able to call loved ones. Even in the darkest times, the sound of a familiar voice could make all the difference.

the first telephone—invented by Alexander Graham Bell

The word *telegraph* comes from the Greek words *tele*, meaning "distant," and *graphein*, which means "to write."

WHICH WORD?

They sound similar, but the words *telegraph*, *telephone*, and *telegram* all refer to different things. *Telegrams* are the printed messages produced by *telegraph* machines. *Telephones* send sound across great distances.

POSTAL TELEGRAPH   COMMERCIAL CABLES

TELEGRAM

transmits and. delivers this message subject to the terms and conditions printed on the back of this blank.

Telegraph-Cable

OUNTER NUMBER.   TIME FILED.

he following message, without repeating, subject ... on the back hereof, which are hereby agreed to,

The telegraph was designed to receive and send one message at a time.

Posthaste

Today, the technology is **obsolete**. But for 150 years, the telegraph machine was an essential tool for news. By the 1920s, sending a telegram was cheaper than making a phone call. Telegraph machines sent electronic signals around the world. The messages announced weddings, births, and deaths. Important news, such as the *Titanic* disaster, was sent by telegraph.

QUICK WIT

Each message was carefully written to be as short as possible. Punctuation cost extra, so it was rarely used. Instead, people wrote *STOP* instead of periods. Pronouns and verbs were avoided.

a young telegram messenger

The last telegram was sent in 2006.

an operator listening
to Morse Code

Morse Code

A •—
B —•••
C —•—•
D —••
E •
F ••—•
G ——•
H ••••
I ••
J •———
K —•—
L •—••

M ——
N —•
O ———
P •——•
Q ——•—
R •—•
S •••
T —
U ••—
V •••—
W •——

Y —•——
Z ——••
Ä •—•—
Ö ———•
Ü ••——
Ch ————
0 —————
1 •————
2 ••———
3 •••——
4 ••••—

6 —••••
7 ——•••
8 ———••
9 ————•
. •—•—•—
, ——••——
? ••——••
! —•—•——
: ———•••
" •—••—•
' •————•
= —•••—

MORSE CODE

The military used telegraphs to report
the news from war zones. The details
were sent by Morse Code. Morse Code
is made up of short and long sounds.
Each group of sounds represents a
letter. When the listener puts together
all the sounds, a message is revealed.
These quick messages helped people
stay informed about the war.

Telephones

In 1876, inventor Alexander Graham Bell shouted to his assistant through the first telephone, "Watson, come here! I want to see you!" These simple words changed lives. Now, people could use a telephone to spread the latest news.

Phones help us stay in touch with friends in distant places. And we can call others to discuss important news. After a disaster, the first thing many people do is call their loved ones. They want to make sure they are safe. That is probably the most important news for many people.

In March 1876, Alexander Graham Bell placed the first telephone call to Thomas A. Watson in the next room.

In 1915, Bell took his invention to the next level. He called Watson again. This time, the call was from New York City to San Francisco.

In 2012, a team of two Latvians placed the longest phone call. The call lasted over 54 hours!

In 1969, President Richard Nixon made a call from Earth to space. He called the astronauts who had just set foot on the moon.

AHOY VS. HELLO

Alexander Graham Bell thought "Ahoy" was the ideal greeting when answering the phone. But Thomas Edison, another great inventor, urged people to say "Hello" instead.

BIGGER BROADCASTS

Newspapers report on events from around the world. They cover politics, fashion, sports, and local news. The most important news is on the front page. The headlines are designed to catch readers' attention and get them to buy a paper.

For years, newspaper was king. Then, radio added another dimension to the story. Radio programs didn't have pictures like newspapers. But the stories felt more emotional. You could hear happiness, excitement, sadness, or fear in someone's voice.

READ ALL ABOUT IT!

Newspapers used to make "extra special" editions during big news events such as a presidential election or a war. Newsboys who sold newspapers on the street corners tried to grab people's attention with their shouts "Extra! Extra! Read all about it!"

POWERFUL SIGNAL

In 1938, *The War of the Worlds* radio program presented fake news bulletins about an alien invasion. At the beginning of the program, an announcement was made that the bulletins were not real. But many people tuned in late. Those people thought it was true. They panicked. Some loaded guns to protect themselves from the aliens. Some hid in their cellars.

an early radio

In the beginning, newspapers were only one page. In 1690, the first newspaper to have more pages upset readers and was shut down after only one printing.

What's the Headline?

Millions started reading newspapers during World War I. And after the war, people continued reading them to keep up with important events. One of the biggest stories began on October 29th, 1929. People called that day "Black Tuesday." Billions of dollars were lost in the **stock market**. People all around the country lost money on that day. Many businesses had to close. And with that, huge numbers of people lost their jobs. People didn't have enough money to buy food. The headlines reported the latest news with big bold letters. The **Great Depression** was major news for many years.

BLACK BLIZZARDS

At first, the Great Depression only concerned people in the cities. But sadly, at the same time, farms were being destroyed by a drought that had hit the middle of the country. This lack of water lasted years. And it was made worse by huge windstorms. These dust storms were so bad that people called them "black blizzards." Witnesses said they turned day to night. By 1940, two million people had been forced to leave their homes.

BROOKLYN DAILY EAGLE
And Complete Long Island News

LATE NEWS

WALL ST. IN PANIC AS STOCKS CR

ttempt Made to Kill Italy's Crown Prince

Hollywood Fire
Destroys Films
Worth Millions

High Duty Group
Gave $700,000 to
Coolidge Drive

YEARS OF DUST

TLEMENT ADMINISTRATION
es Victims
es Land to Proper Use

VOL. LXXIX....No. 26,206.

RICES OF STOCKS CRASH
IN HEAVY LIQUIDATION,
TOTAL DROP OF BILLIONS

PAPER LOSS $4,000,000,000

2,600,000 Shares Sold
in the Final Hour in
Record Decline.

MANY ACCOUNTS WIPED OUT

But No Brokerage House Is in
Difficulties, as Margins Have
Been Kept High.

ORGANIZED BACKING ABSEN

Thyroid Determines if a Man
Should Be Flier, Says Dr. Asher

Special to The New York Times.
BALTIMORE, Md., Oct. 23.—
Upon perfect thyroid condi

LASTING MEMORIES

Newspaper articles and
photographs show what the Great
Depression was like. People had
dramatic stories to tell about their
experiences. Newspapers recorded
their stories. And today, reading
them can help us understand the
history of our country.

Worth a Thousand Words

It is said a picture is worth a thousand words. People snapped plenty of pictures of men and women returning from World War II. The most famous photo was taken at a parade in New York City. It was published in a 1945 issue of *Life* magazine. The photo showed a sailor kissing a nurse. It became the symbol of the joy people felt at the end of the war. When people saw that image, they knew the war was over in a way that felt more real than simply reading about it.

Honolulu Star-Bulletin 1st EXTRA

8 PAGES— HONOLULU, TERRITORY OF HAWAII, U.S.A., SUNDAY, DECEMBER 7, 1941—8 PAGES · PRICE FIVE CENTS

(Associated Press by Transpacific Telephone)

SAN FRANCISCO, Dec. 7.—President Roosevelt announced this morning that Japanese planes had attacked Manila and Pearl Harbor.

WAR!
OAHU BOM
JAPANES

SIX KNOWN DEAD, 21 INJURED

Attack Made On Island's Defense Areas

THE BEGINNING AND THE END

Newspapers printed stories about the major events of World War II. When they reported the bombing of Pearl Harbor, they helped convince people the United States should enter the war. About two and a half years later, newspapers told of D-Day. That was when Allied Forces made a surprise attack on the beaches of Normandy, France. That successful attack led to the end of the war.

The end of the war was captured with this powerful image.

REPORTING TROUBLE

Today, newspapers don't just report on trouble—they *are* in trouble. Printed papers aren't as popular as they used to be, and they're struggling to make money. People use other faster media to learn about the latest events. Newspapers are fighting to survive by publishing unique and thoughtful articles that can't be found anywhere else.

Dig Deeper!

Hot Headlines

Whether they are on magazines, blogs, or newspapers, headlines are the first things most people read when looking for the latest news. So what's the secret to getting all eyeballs on your story? Check out the tips below to learn how to write a powerful headline that will get the world excited to read about your latest news.

DISCOVER THE WORLD OF ARCHERY!

Engage readers with a verb.

School Gets Out Two Hours Early!

Be direct.

Explain how the story is useful.

Ask a question that demands an answer.

How to Make a Million Dollars

5% off if you are buyer, Certified and Licensed home inspector. Call Now for 280$

2 bed condo charm Now

★ ★ ★ ★ ★ MORTGAGE SOLUTIONS!

Keep it brief.

Are Girls Smarter than Boys?

Hope Lives!

Fireside Chats

Life during the wars was difficult. Food and fuel were in short supply. And many loved ones were in danger. Families gathered around the radio to listen to the news. President Franklin D. Roosevelt spoke to Americans in radio **addresses** called Fireside Chats. He tried to ease their concerns. Nearly 40 years later, President Ronald Reagan continued the tradition. Since then, the president has given a weekly address. In keeping with the times, President Barack Obama uses video addresses that can be viewed online.

THE NEW DEAL

President Roosevelt had a plan for America. He called it the **New Deal**. He wanted the government to help people by ending the Great Depression. Much like today, people couldn't agree on how to help the country. Roosevelt used his Fireside Chats to convince people to support his New Deal.

Radio Everywhere

Today, we have our favorite shows on TV. Before TVs were invented, American homes had radios. People listened to the same kinds of programs that are on TV today. Some people loved news programs, and others liked dramas, comedy, and music. So what has changed? The technology, not the people!

Alerting the Public

Today, many people still listen to the radio for news and entertainment. The radio is also a powerful way to send messages during emergencies. If TVs or Internet channels are destroyed in a storm or military attack, radio signals may still be able to announce the latest events and safety instructions.

ON THE BIG SCREEN

It's hard to imagine a time when television and movies weren't a part of daily life. Before the 1960s, people didn't have TVs in their homes. They couldn't pop in a DVD to watch their favorite movie. But they could learn about current news events during a visit to the local movie theater.

Moving Pictures

By the 1890s, the motion-picture projector was invented. A light shone through a strip of film as it turned on a reel. These moving pictures were magnified onto a screen for audiences to watch. During World War II, people didn't have TVs in their homes. So for news and entertainment, people went to the movies. Newsreels were shown before the movies. They told people what was happening in the war. They also explained how people could ration supplies at home to make life easier for the soldiers.

PROPAGANDA

During the war, it was important for soldiers to have what they needed. So people had to ration, or give up, some things. The government used **propaganda** to convince them it was the right thing to do. Propaganda uses emotional images and messages to convince someone of something.

"We are saving you
YOU save FOOD"

Well fed Soldiers
WILL WIN the WAR

THE FIRST MOVIE THEATER

If you lived in Pittsburgh, Pennsylvania, in 1905, you could ask your mom and dad to take you to the grand opening of the Nickelodeon. It was the first place built just to show movies. It could seat 96 people. And you could watch movies all day for a nickel.

Eyes on the Sky

By 1960, 85 percent of American homes had a TV. On a summer evening in 1969, families sat in front of their black-and-white TVs. They were waiting to see something special. The images were grainy. The sound was fuzzy and difficult to hear. But all across America, people felt united as they watched Neil Armstrong walk on the surface of the moon.

SEEING IS BELIEVING

Landing a man on the moon would have been an amazing accomplishment at any moment in history. But if people had only been able to hear the reports over the radio, it might not have been as memorable. Seeing Armstrong walk on the moon made the event even more exciting. People could imagine they were right there with him in a way that might not have been possible with radio.

A Giant Leap

While Neil Armstrong walked on the moon, he talked to people on Earth. As he took his first steps on the moon, he said "That's one small step for man; one giant leap for mankind."

The Televised War

By the late 1960s, most Americans had access to news around the world. They enjoyed reading newspapers every morning. In the evenings, they could watch the news on TV. And in the 60s, news of the Vietnam War had people glued to their sets. It was the first war to be shown on TV. War **correspondents** reported directly from the battle sites. People saw soldiers shot before their eyes. The war felt closer and more important because people could watch it happening on TV.

VIETNAM PROTESTS

By being shown on TV, the war seemed to touch people personally. Hundreds of people spoke out against the Vietnam War. There were many marches and rallies. The Vietnam protest movement became one of the largest anti-war protests in United States history. Some people believe there was so much outrage over the Vietnam War because of the TV coverage.

Protestors face policemen outside the Great Hall of the People in Tiananmen Square in Beijing.

TIANANMEN SQUARE

America isn't the only place that has protestors. In 1989, student protestors occupied Tiananmen Square in Beijing, China. They wanted more rights. One man stood up in front of a line of military tanks. Newspapers around the world carried a photo of it. It became the image that pushed the world to ask China for political change.

Skewed News

Today, people are fascinated with the lives of famous people. Knowing this, some news outlets focus on celebrities. The **paparazzi** get paid a lot of money to find out personal details about famous people. To learn the latest, they often invade celebrities' privacy. Many of these reporters are more interested in making money than being accurate. So their stories are often untrue or exaggerated.

ROYAL WEDDINGS

England still has a royal family. And like any family, they have weddings. These royal weddings are spectacular events. In 2012, Prince William married Catherine Middleton. Millions of people watched their wedding on television. And over 72 million people watched it on YouTube.

PAPARAZZI

Many celebrities do not like the paparazzi. They believe the paparazzi go too far to get the photographs or information they want. Some paparazzi do dangerous and illegal things to get the scoop. They may go through a star's garbage, climb fences, or chase cars to get pictures.

REAL-TIME NEWS

People no longer need to wait a month or even a day to get the news. Now, news is announced in **real-time** almost as soon as it happens. TV programs and web pages deliver the news around the clock. And as technology continues to grow, the news will find us in unique ways. One day, perhaps news will be sent directly to our brains!

THE CELL PHONE

The first cell phones were larger than home phones, and they did nothing but place calls. Now cell phones report the news, search the Internet, take photos, send emails, play games, and make phone calls.

CNN

The Cable News Network (CNN) was the first 24-hour television station that did nothing but deliver news. CNN was founded and started broadcasting in 1980. Its headquarters is in Atlanta, Georgia. The channel is broadcast in over 150 countries.

September 11th

On a clear Tuesday morning in 2001, disaster struck in New York City. News reports showed planes striking the city's famous Twin Towers. Around the world, people watched in horror. Soon after, the buildings collapsed, and a cloud of dust fell over the city.

People were desperate for information. The planes had been taken over by **terrorists** who wanted to show how much they hated American culture. The day was sealed in the memories of millions of people. But with real-time news, people were able to respond quickly.

A MEMORIAL

The buildings may no longer be there, but a memorial was made in their place. It honors the more than 2,000 people who died that day. The museum contains news items, photographs, audio, and videos of people's reactions to the devastating event.

TWIN TOWERS

The Twin Towers were two 110-story buildings located on the island of Manhattan. The buildings had long been considered a symbol of the financial power of the United States. By destroying the buildings, the terrorists were trying to tell the world the United States wasn't as powerful as others believed it to be.

On-the-scene reporters captured images of victims covered in ash and debris.

Social Media

Today, **social media** is used in almost every part of our lives. We talk to friends on Facebook. We read about what movie stars are up to on Twitter. And on YouTube, we watch videos made by people around the world. This is how we stay connected. And it's also how we get much of our news.

Journalists have strict rules about what they can talk about. But social media sites don't have these rules. People can talk about anything they want. In some ways this is dangerous. It means things that aren't true can be presented as fact. But social media has helped people share news in countries where TV and radio are controlled by the government. Websites like Facebook and Twitter have even helped spark revolutions.

JOURNALISM

Unlike writers on social-media sites, journalists are supposed to write without **bias**. That means journalists should only report the facts and not their personal opinions. This allows people reading the story to get all the facts and form their own opinions.

SOUND BITES

Imagine if we had social media years ago. A few lines here or there might not have changed history, but we'll never know!

Dr. Martin Luther King, Jr. @MLK_Jr

Hope to see you all at my rally tomorrow, August 28th. #IHaveADream

Paul Revere @on_horseback

Hey guys, the British are coming! repost. #RedCoats

Sacagawea @Guides_R_Us

Heading west with @Lewis and @Clark. I found a great shortcut! #ThruTheRockies

Amelia Earhart @LadyLindy

We ran out of gas flying over the Pacific. Can someone give us a lift off this dinky island? #AroundtheWorld

DIG DEEPER!

BUTTON BREAKDOWN

A wave of revolutions happened in 2011. In many Middle Eastern and North African countries, the people rose up against their leaders. They called for a new, fairer government. These revolutions had their roots in social media. And unlike much of the news, the postings on social media could not be controlled or edited by the government. In places like Egypt, this meant that activists could organize a revolution. It was powerful enough to get rid of a ruler who unfairly dominated the country for 30 years.

Postings on Facebook and Twitter told the time and place of protests.

Videos, photographs, and maps were easily shared to keep activists engaged and organized.

All these devices made it easier for protestors to keep in touch and react.

FORECASTING THE FUTURE

It can be printed or online. We can hear it on the radio or on our phones. Good or bad, news is all around us. It connects people around the world. The knowledge it provides empowers us to change the world. And whatever form it takes, there will always be new stories to tell.

ALL KINDS OF NEWS

News isn't always serious and sad. Some of the most popular news stories are ones of great joy. Stories of royal marriages, people rescuing others, or amazing feats of strength are also news items that people want to know about.

GLOSSARY

abolitionists—people who believe slavery should be illegal

addresses—prepared speeches delivered to special audiences or on special occasions

artifacts—objects representing people or periods from the past

bias—an attitude that favors one way of feeling or acting over any other

Confederacy—the name given to the southern states that wanted to form their own country during the Civil War

consistent—regular or dependable

correspondents—reporters who deliver news from a foreign country

editorials—newspaper or magazine articles that give the opinions of the editors or publishers

Great Depression—the economic crisis and period of low business activity in the United States and other countries, beginning with the stock market crash in 1929, and continuing through most of the 1930s

journalists—writers or editors for newspapers, magazines, and radio or television news programs

literacy—the ability to read and write

local—nearby a particular place

New Deal—the policies of President Franklin D. Roosevelt, developed to grow the United States economy after the Great Depression

obsolete—no longer in use or no longer useful

orally—related to the spoken word

pamphlet—a small publication, usually 80 pages or less, on a single topic

paparazzi—people who aggressively photograph or write about famous people

pessimistic—looks at the negative parts of something; always expects the worst

propaganda—ideas or statements, which are often exaggerated or false, that are spread to help a cause

real-time—the same time in which something is happening

social media—electronic forms of communication through which users share information and opinions

stock market—a place where much of the money of a country is traded

terrorists —people who use violent acts to frighten others as a way of trying to achieve a political goal

truce—an agreement between groups to stop fighting

vital—something of great importance

INDEX

BIBLIOGRAPHY

Dubowski, Mark. *Titanic: The Disaster that Shocked the World!* **DK Readers, 2012.**

Full of facts and details about the *Titanic*, this book will be hard to put down. Find out how the world learned about this terrible disaster.

Ross, Stewart. *The Home Front in World War II (History Through Newspapers).* **Wayland Publishing Limited, 2003.**

This book uses real newspaper articles from World War II to bring the period to life. Each article helps you practice evaluating reliable sources.

Schwartz, Heather E. *Yourspace: Questioning New Media.* **Capstone Press, 2008.**

You can't believe everything you read. Learn to question media and better evaluate the sources you'll come across in daily life.

Tarshis, Lauren. *I Survived the Attacks of September 11th, 2001.* **Scholastic Paperbacks, 2012.**

This is a story of a boy caught in New York City the day of the September 11th attack. Follow him as he searches for his father, a New York City firefighter.

MORE TO EXPLORE

TIME for Kids
http://www.timeforkids.com/news

Stay up to date on current and unforgettable news events written
just for you. You'll get everything from sports and entertainment to
national and world news.

What Happened? The Story of September 11th
*http://www.nick.com/videos/clip/nick-news-what-happened-the-true-story-
of-september-11th-full-episode.html*

Nicknews.com covered the facts of the September 11th tragedy.
You'll find interviews from kids and public figures near the World
Trade Center and get a clearer understanding of the events of this
unforgettable day.

Fun English Games
http://www.funenglishgames.com/writinggames/newspaper.html

Learn how to write a great newspaper headline. Read various
headings and decide how the heading could be improved. When
you are finished, you can practice writing your own headlines..

How to Learn Morse Code
http://www.learnmorsecode.info/

Get tips and tricks for learning Morse Code. You'll even find a
video of a boy who is learning to communicate fully through
Morse Code.

ABOUT THE AUTHOR

Tamara Leigh Hollingsworth was born and raised in Cupertino, California. She attended Hollins University, an all-women's college, in Roanoke, Virginia, where she earned a degree in English. While in college, she spent time traveling through Europe. For the majority of her life since then, she has been a high school English teacher. She currently lives in Atlanta, Georgia. When she's not working with her beloved students, Tamara loves to spend time with her husband, her daughter, and her books. She reads an online newspaper every day.